Know Yourself
to
Love Yourself

BRITTANY M. ROBINSON

Copyright © 2022 BRITTANY M. ROBINSON
All rights reserved.

ACKNOWLEDGMENTS

Having an idea and turning it into a book is as hard as it sounds. The experience is both internally challenging and rewarding.

I especially want to thank the individuals that helped make this happen. The world is a better place thanks to people who want to develop and lead others. What makes it even better are people who share the gift of their time to mentor future leaders

Self-love is knowing your own self and the value of yourself.

There are many levels of self-love that one must go through to come to love oneself truly and constantly.

The road to self-love is one filled with effort, perseverance and hundreds of conversations with internal struggles that must be had in order to finally reach the happiness and inner peace that comes from deeply loving oneself.

Knowing the value that you have as a person, you know what you are and you understand that you should not demand anything from anyone because everything you need is inside you. This is because you are a complete being that is full of good things, positive vibes and energies, qualities and virtues that make you enough to achieve what you dream of, what you deserve, what you propose and much more. By loving yourself, you understand that and you are aware of your inner power. It doesn't get any better than that.

Also, by loving yourself you understand that you should not ask anyone or seek outside information about who you are because no one will understand more about yourself than you do, no one will know more about yourself and only you control everything that is inside of you.

If you have doubts, problems or internal worries, you must work to know yourself much more and thus dissipate that which once clouded you to have your life clear and feel full with what you are. That is why self-love is to understand that only you understand, comprehend and know in depth what is in you, what you can do and what you need to improve.

Self-love is also to bring out everything that is inside you, regardless of whether it is good or bad in our eyes, understanding that everything you have is part of who you are and that you should be proud of it, work on it and learn along the way.

To love oneself is to build and rebuild oneself constantly being aware of what one feels for oneself, understanding oneself from the inside to the outside and managing all that we are and want to be in order to build the basis of self-love and a deep knowledge of oneself.

Accepting oneself, one has confidence in what one does, grows and learns, and understanding that life is centered on these two bases. It is then understood that, by loving oneself, one lives a happy and fulfilled life.

Knowing that one is beautiful in all the different and incredible ways we are, we understand that we deserve happiness and love to reign in our lives. In addition, we open the door to encounter abundance and prosperity, as well as self-confidence and positive energies.

Self-love is then, doing things by and for yourself, giving yourself the love you deserve, dedicating time to love yourself, to understand what is inside you. Understanding your strengths, weaknesses and even knowing your limits and sharing them with others so that they respect them and consequently, that they respect you. In this sense, to love yourself is to always remember that we should not allow others to depress us with criticism or ill-intentioned actions because they are external people to us and do not have the power or the right to intervene in our lives and pretend to change the ideas of who we are.

It is common to see how many people spread negative energies around the world, looking down on others, criticizing and filling themselves and others with negative thoughts about others. Regardless of whether they are friends or family, these people thrive on hurting others, giving up living their lives to criticize others. It is difficult to understand that they are the ones who are wrong and not us, because sometimes society makes us think that we should love everyone, although this is not the case. When you love yourself, you understand that these things are not important and you also understand that these types of people should not be in your life because they simply do not deserve it.

When you love yourself, you are able to exercise a limit and leave behind all the negative vibes and people that surround you, achieving then, to live in peace and tranquility with those who are and with those who are gone from your life because you understand that no matter who they are or what happened with them, it is something that happened that way for a special reason and because their presence or absence in your life makes you grow and be better.

Having self-awareness, we are able to speak and control what comes out of our mouth, making it only words of approval and love for ourselves. We become people who do not have negative energies towards others because we take care of ourselves and live a full, happy and peaceful life with who we are.

When our energies are not clear, it is necessary to make a pause that allows us to clarify ourselves, listening to our inner self and understanding what we are to clarify ourselves and heal our wounds to move forward, understanding what is within us and understanding that we are beings of light and good.

Psychology is changing, the way we want to be loved and cared for is transforming and it is because as individual beings that belong to a large society, we are understanding that we must make a change to look for what we really need. We are beings under construction and now psychology understands this.

It is now much clearer to us that what really deserves our attention and who really deserves to be in our lives must be a reflection of our true selves.

Change can only come from within us because our improvements cannot depend on anyone else and that is something we must understand because we are not meant to be perfect.

We are beings that make mistakes and that is something we should also be grateful for, for it is mistakes that make us grow, learn and forge our path of goodness.

It is only by loving ourselves that we will love our life, our successes, our failures and above all, our past, present and future.

After reading these words, it is good that you make an introspection to understand yourself much better and begin your journey towards self-love.

1. Who are you?

2. Do you think you have been loving yourself throughout your life?

2. *Do you have any ties to the past?*

4. *What do you need to change to really love yourself?*

5. Make a list of the weaknesses you hope to transform.

6. *Make a list of your greatest strengths*

7. What words define you?

8. What goals do you have for your life?

9. What does your inner self say about you?

10. Now tell yourself everything you have been wanting to hear all this time. Form love-filled messages to yourself.

It's time to forge your own path to self-love, friend. Find your own self. Be free to be you, be free to love yourself and be free to enjoy this process.

ABOUT THE AUTHOR

I have been married since 2008, and I met my husband in 2006.

I had to teach myself self-love and self-worth. I was in my 20s when I got married, so it was a challenge.

I had to teach myself how to balance's self-love. So, I had to understand what I wanted and needed. I had to learn the value of myself. I had to learn how to deal with friends and family on different levels in my life.

Now I have four children. I'm in my late 30, so I put who I want around them. It is all about balance, self-love, value yourself, recharging yourself, and confidence in your own reflections with your family. I know from personal experiences that it was rough and hard, but when I started doing it, it was a smooth road now.

www.ingramcontent.com/pod-product-compliance
Lightning Source LLC
Chambersburg PA
CBHW042129160426
43198CB00021B/2949